World History & Cultures

Discovering Ancient Greece

by
Wendy Frey

Don Johnston Incorporated
Volo, Illinois

Edited by:

John Bergez
Start-to-Finish Core Content Series Editor, Pacifica, California

Gail Portnuff Venable, MS, CCC-SLP
Speech/Language Pathologist, San Francisco, California

Dorothy Tyack, MA
Learning Disabilities Specialist, San Francisco, California

Jerry Stemach, MS, CCC-SLP
Speech/Language Pathologist, Director of Content Development, Sonoma County, California

Graphics and Illustrations:

Photographs and illustrations are all created professionally
and modified to provide the best possible support for the
intended reader.
Pages 6: Library of Congress, Prints and Photographs Division [LC-USZ62-116781]
Pages 13, 47: © akg-images / Peter Connolly
Pages 19: Library of Congress, Prints and Photographs Division [LC-USZ62-66132]
Pages 44: Library of Congress, Prints and Photographs Division [LC-USZ62-60980]
Pages 55: © AP/WideWorldPhotos
All other photos © Don Johnston Incorporated and its licensors.

Narration:

Professional actors and actresses read the text to build
excitement and to model research-based elements of fluency:
intonation, stress, prosody, phrase groupings and rate.
The rate has been set to maximize comprehension for the reader.

Published by:

Don Johnston Incorporated
26799 West Commerce Drive
Volo, IL 60073

800.999.4660 USA Canada
800.889.5242 Technical Support
www.donjohnston.com

International Standard Book Number
ISBN 1-4105-0456-5

Table of Contents

Ancient Greece

How long ago was ancient Greece? Look at the timeline on this page. It shows some of the events that you will read about in this book.

On the timeline, we count forward from the year 1 A.D. to get up to today. There have been a little more than 2000 years since 1 A.D. When we are not writing about ancient times, we usually leave off the A.D. and just write the number of the year.

Years that come before 1 A.D. are always marked B.C. We count backward from the year 1 B.C. to get to the very ancient past. For instance, the timeline shows that the Trojan War took place in about 1200 B.C. That is 1200 years before 1 A.D., or about 3200 years ago in all.

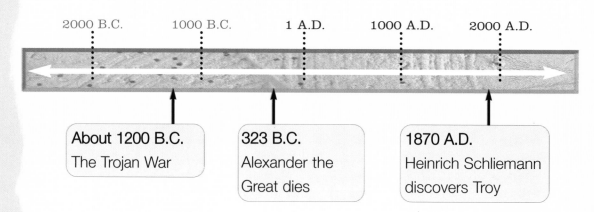

| 2000 B.C. | 1000 B.C. | 1 A.D. | 1000 A.D. | 2000 A.D. |

About 1200 B.C.
The Trojan War

323 B.C.
Alexander the
Great dies

1870 A.D.
Heinrich Schliemann
discovers Troy

Introduction: Detectives of the Past

When Heinrich Schliemann was a boy, back in the 1830s, he loved stories about ancient Greece. He loved hearing about the god Zeus and his family, and he loved the story of how the Olympic Games began. But Heinrich's favorite story was the story of the Trojan War. This was the tale of a fierce struggle between the Greeks and the Trojans. The Trojans lived across the sea from Greece. The war happened many centuries ago, probably around 1200 B.C.

According to ancient Greek stories, the war began when a Trojan prince ran away with a beautiful Greek queen named Helen.

The Trojans lived in the city of Troy, across the sea from Greece.

5

The Greeks raised a great army and followed the Trojans to their home, the city of Troy. For ten years, the Greeks tried to enter the city and capture Troy, and for ten years, the Trojans fought to keep them out. The Greeks finally won and burned Troy to the ground.

Because the city of Troy was gone, many people thought the Trojan War was just a story. But young Heinrich believed that the story was true, and he wanted to find the lost city of Troy.

Heinrich grew up and married a Greek woman named Sophia. Together, Heinrich and Sophia set out to search for Troy. They knew this would not be an easy mission since more than 3000 years had passed since the Trojan War. To find clues, they turned to the stories Heinrich had loved so much as a boy. Heinrich had learned about the Trojan War from two long poems written by an ancient Greek author named Homer. The poems were called the *Iliad* and the *Odyssey*. Heinrich and Sophia studied these poems carefully. They searched for the names of places and tried to figure out where the city of Troy had once stood.

Heinrich Schliemann

In 1870, Heinrich and Sophia traveled to Turkey to follow up on clues they had found in the poems. They went to a hill called *Hissarlik*, which means "the palace" in Turkish. The hill was close to the Aegean Sea, across the water from Greece. Heinrich and Sophia hired workers to help them, and they started to dig.

Heinrich and Sophia found many things as they dug. They found parts of ancient walls. They found objects like jars and pitchers. They were excited to see that the walls and the objects were very, very old. In time, historians would agree that Heinrich had found the ancient city of Troy. His boyhood dream had come true.

Heinrich and Sophia were true detectives of the past. They solved the mystery of Troy by following clues and searching for evidence in a scientific way.

Since then, many other detectives of the past have followed in their footsteps. Most of them have been **archeologists**. Archeologists are scientists who study things that were left behind by people who lived a long time ago. In this book, we will join archeologists in searching for clues about life in ancient Greece. We will investigate an ancient temple, city walls, a helmet, a public square, and a coin.

Chapter One

Gods and Goddesses

Questions this chapter will answer:

- **What were ancient Greek temples like?**

- **What gods and goddesses did the Greeks believe in?**

- **How did the Greeks try to keep the gods happy?**

A Greek temple as it looks today

Look at this picture. It shows an ancient temple that sits on top of a steep hill in the city of Athens, Greece. The temple is called the Parthenon. Some parts of the building are missing, but you can see its marble columns from almost everywhere in Athens. Could this temple hold clues to what life was like in ancient Greece? This is what an archeologist would try to find out.

Archeologists try to understand the past by investigating the objects people have made and left behind. These objects are called **artifacts**. Ancient buildings like the Parthenon are artifacts, and so are weapons, pottery, coins, and art. When archeologists find an artifact, they examine it carefully. They ask questions like, *Who owned this object? How was it used? What can it teach us about the people who made it?*

9

Athens is a wonderful place for discovering the past. It is full of artifacts that were left behind by the ancient Greeks. Some of these artifacts have been dug out of the ground and are now on display in museums. Old **ruins** (buildings that have been partly destroyed) can still be found out in the open.

What can we learn about ancient Greece by walking through the ruins of a temple? Let's find out by visiting the Parthenon.

This ancient Greek jug is on display in a museum.

A Perfect Home for a Goddess

The Parthenon is on a hill called the Acropolis, which means "high city" in Greek. The ancient Greeks built three temples on the hill. The biggest and most beautiful one was the Parthenon.

As we look at the ruins of the Parthenon, we can imagine what it looked like long ago. The Greeks used white marble to build the temple. When it was new, it sparkled in the sun. They also painted parts of the temple in bright colors. The roof was slanted to make two triangles, one in front and one in back. Under the roof, and inside the triangles, were sculptures of gods and goddesses. We can also see scenes that have been carved into the marble. These scenes tell stories about the gods. When we talk about the gods in this book, we're really talking about goddesses, too.

The Parthenon looked like this in ancient times.

This scene was carved into one of the walls of the Parthenon. It shows three of the Greek gods.

The Greeks worked hard to make their temples beautiful because they built them to honor their gods and goddesses. They also built them as earthly homes for the gods.

Usually, the Greeks built a temple for one special god or goddess. The people of Athens built the Parthenon for Athena, the goddess of wisdom and learning, because they believed that she protected their city.

11

A huge statue of Athena stood inside the temple. The statue isn't there any more, but we know about it from the writings of ancient travelers who saw it. The statue was made by a man named Phidias, who was one of the best sculptors in Athens. He built a wooden frame that was almost 40 feet tall and covered it with gold and ivory. The people of Athens liked the statue, but they were annoyed that Phidias had carved a picture of his own face into the shield that he had put into Athena's hand.

A Family of Gods and Goddesses

The ancient Greeks believed in many gods and goddesses. They believed that their gods looked like people, except that they were bigger, stronger, and more beautiful than people. And, unlike people, the gods were immortal (they lived forever).

The Greeks told colorful stories about the gods. The stories are called myths. The Greeks used these myths to try to understand and explain their world. According to the Greek myths, 12 of the gods and goddesses lived on Mount Olympus. There really is a mountain in Greece called Mount Olympus, but it's only 9,550 feet (2,911 meters) high, and that's a fairly easy climb. The Mount Olympus in Greek myths was higher than any human could climb.

The ancient Greeks thought that their gods lived like a family. Zeus was the king of all the gods. His wife was named Hera. Zeus had many children. His favorite child was Athena.

This statue is a full-sized model of Phidias's statue of Athena. The statue towered over the people who visited the Parthenon.

The story of Athena's birth is a strange one. One day, Zeus had a terrible headache that kept getting worse and worse. Then, just when he thought he couldn't take the pain another minute, a crack opened in his head, and out jumped Athena. She was already a grown woman, and she was wearing **armor** (pieces of metal that are worn for protection in battles).

The Greeks believed that the family of gods controlled everything, from the movement of the sun to the daily lives of every person. Each god or goddess was responsible for one or two areas of life. For example, Zeus's brother, Poseidon, was the god of the seas. Poseidon had a beard that was the color of the ocean. Zeus's son, Apollo, was the god of the sun. Apollo drove across the sky in a glowing **chariot** (a cart that was pulled by horses).

A statue of Poseidon

Prayers, Sacrifices, and Festivals

Because the gods were so powerful, the ancient Greeks felt it was important to make them happy. The Greeks believed that if the gods were unhappy, they might punish people by doing things like sending storms to destroy their crops.

The Greeks did many things to make Zeus and his family happy. They carved statues of the gods and goddesses, and they built temples for them, like the Parthenon. They prayed to the gods. They gave them gifts of food, wine, pottery, and gold. Sometimes the Greeks **sacrificed** animals such as goats, sheep, and pigs. This means they killed the animals and gave them to the gods. The Greeks also held many festivals to honor the gods. Festivals included prayers and sacrifices. They also included sporting events. Remember, the Greeks believed that the gods were like people in many ways. Therefore, they thought the gods would enjoy many of the same things people enjoyed.

The **Olympic Games** were the largest sporting event in ancient Greece. They were held to honor Zeus, in a place called Olympia. The events at the Olympic Games were similar to the events we have today.

In ancient times, fans walked through this entrance to get to the Olympic Games.

They included wrestling, boxing, foot races, and javelin (spear) throwing. The games in ancient Greece also included some events we don't have today, such as chariot races. The Olympics were so important to the Greeks that they stopped all wars during the time the games were held. They wanted to make sure that athletes from all over Greece could travel safely to the games.

© Dimitri Iundr/CORBIS

Throwing the javelin is still an Olympic sport today.

Chapter Summary

In this chapter, you visited the Parthenon to learn about the gods and goddesses of ancient Greece. Archeologists have learned a lot about ancient Greek religion by studying Greek myths and the ruins of temples. Through their investigations, we know that the Greeks worshipped many gods. They built temples to the gods, and they honored the gods with prayers, sacrifices, and festivals. The Olympic Games that we know today began as a festival to honor Zeus.

The ancient Greeks built temples and held festivals to honor their gods and goddesses. These activities were also a way to show how proud they were of their cities. What were these cities like? In the next chapter, you will learn more about ancient Greek cities.

Chapter Two

City-States

Questions this chapter will answer:

• **What was a Greek city-state?**

• **How was Sparta different from other Greek city-states?**

• **What was the city-state of Athens famous for?**

In many parts of Greece, you can find parts of ancient stone walls. The Greeks made their walls using large and small stones, and bricks that were made out of mud. In some places the stones make beautiful patterns. The walls give us clues about how the ancient Greeks lived.

Archeologists have discovered that the Greeks built strong walls around many of their cities. Some of these walls were 10 feet thick and 25 feet tall. They had square towers every few feet where lookouts could stand and watch for danger. There were gates in the walls to let people in and out of the city.

This picture shows the ruins of an ancient wall. The wall was built to protect a Greek city.

One reason people build walls is to protect themselves and keep others out. If you looked at the ruins of these strong walls, you might guess that ancient Greek cities fought wars with each other. Writings and other artifacts show that this guess would be correct. In fact, ancient Greece was not one country, like the United States or England. Instead, ancient Greece was made up of **city-states**, each with its own government, its own army, and its own ways of life. In this chapter you'll find out how these city-states came to be, and what they were like.

From Farms to City-States

Greece is surrounded by the Mediterranean Sea and the Aegean Sea. It is a land of steep mountains and hills. There is not a lot of flat land.

This Greek town is built on the side of a steep hill.

The early Greeks were farmers. They lived on farms or in small villages near the sea or between the mountains. Over time, the villages grew larger and became small cities. An ancient Greek city included a settlement surrounded by walls and the farmland outside the walls.

The steep mountains made travel between cities difficult, so the cities never came together to form one country.

Instead, each city had its own government, its own army, and its own coins of silver or gold. The Greeks believed that each city had its own god or goddess to protect it, as Athena protected Athens. In many ways, ancient Greek cities were like very small countries. That is why we call them city-states.

Two of the most powerful city-states were Sparta and Athens. There was less than 100 miles between these two city-states, but the people who lived in them had very different ways of life.

Athens and Sparta were less than 100 miles apart.

In fact, there was no love between Sparta and Athens, and they fought a number of wars with each other. Let's visit these two city-states and find out more about them.

Sparta: A City of Soldiers

Sparta was in the southern part of Greece, on flat farmland between the mountains and the sea. The Spartans did not build walls around their city because they didn't need them. They had such a strong army that they were able to defeat most of the people around them.

Sparta was different from other city-states because the whole city was organized for war. The Spartans put all their energy into creating a great army. They did not worry about decorating their clothes or their buildings. They did not care very much about discovering new ideas. What they cared about was winning wars. The Spartans used war to gain farmland to feed the city. Winning wars also allowed them to make their enemies into slaves.

Sparta was ruled by a small group of men. This group included two kings, who were also generals, and 28 other men from wealthy families. These men made all the big decisions for Sparta, including whether or not to go to war.

In Sparta, both boys and girls were trained to fight. Their training began when they were very young. Spartan boys left home at the age of seven and lived together in groups during their training. When they grew up, they served the city as soldiers. Girls lived at home, but, like boys, they had wrestling matches, foot races, gymnastics, and sword fights.

Spartan boys in training

Athens: A City of New Ideas

Ancient Athens was a walled city a few miles from the Aegean Sea. On the shore of the Aegean Sea near Athens was the port of Ostea. Many ships sailed in and out of this busy port. Many people traveled to Athens from other parts of Greece and the Mediterranean Sea. They brought new goods and new ideas with them. People in Athens liked to talk about important ideas and questions.

All the new ideas made Athens a lively city. Athens became especially famous for new ideas in art and government.

Many artists came to live in Athens. They made beautiful things, including statues and buildings. They also made the best pottery in ancient Greece. The Greeks used pottery for cooking and for storing food and wine. The artists of Athens painted scenes from daily life on the bowls, vases, and other objects they made. Athens traded its beautiful pottery and other goods to people around the Mediterranean Sea. In return, the city got things it needed, such as wheat. Athens grew large and strong from trade.

The scenes on this pottery were painted in ancient Athens.

A new form of government began in Athens. It was called **democracy**, from the Greek word demos, which means "the people." A democracy is ruled by its **citizens**. A citizen is someone who lives in a city or country and has rights there.

In Athens, women were not allowed to be citizens. Slaves were not citizens, either.

To be a citizen, you had to be a man, you had to be free, and you had to have been born in Athens. Every citizen got a vote when it was time to make new laws or choose leaders. Athens was the first place in the world where ordinary people got to say what they thought and to decide important issues. In this way, Athens set an example for future democracies, including our own.

Chapter Summary

In this chapter, you learned about ancient Greek city-states. Thick ancient walls show that the city-states needed protection from each other. Greek city-states were like small countries with their own armies.

Sparta and Athens were two important city-states. Sparta was organized around fighting wars. Athens is famous because of its art and because it is the place where democracy was born. Athens and Sparta were often enemies, and they fought many wars with each other. In the next chapter, you will learn what war was like in ancient Greece. You will also find out how Athens and Sparta came together to fight an enemy from outside Greece.

Chapter Three

The Greeks at War

Questions this chapter will answer:

- Who fought as soldiers in ancient Greece?

- What kinds of weapons and armor did Greek soldiers use?

- Why were the Persian Wars important?

Imagine that you have been digging where Sparta once stood, looking for objects the Spartans may have left behind. You come upon the artifact in the picture on this page. If you guessed that it is a helmet, you are correct. An ancient Greek soldier wore this helmet to protect his head when he went to war.

What do you think this artifact is?

War was part of everyday life in ancient Greece. City-states often fought each other, just as countries do today. But they also banded together to fight an outside enemy — Persia. In this chapter, you'll find out what war was like for the ancient Greeks, and what happened when Persia tried to invade Greece.

Ancient Greek Soldiers

In ancient Greece, most wars were fought by small armies of soldiers on foot. Greek foot soldiers were called hoplites. This word comes from the Greek word *hoplon*, which means "shield." Each hoplite carried a round shield on his left arm and a spear in his right hand. Soldiers often decorated their shields with pictures that would scare the enemy.

Hoplites fought in a small group called a **phalanx**. In a phalanx, the soldiers lined up next to each other, in four to eight rows. They stood so close together that their shields overlapped. In this way, a soldier's shield protected not only himself but also the soldier on his left side. A soldier had to trust his fellow soldiers to protect him.

A hoplite

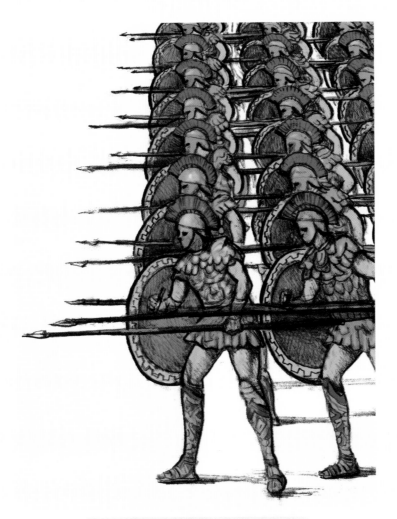

The soldiers in a Greek phalanx
were bunched tightly together.

Most Greek hoplites came from wealthy
families because the hoplites had to pay for
their own weapons and armor. In Sparta,
though, all male citizens were soldiers, not just
the wealthy men.

29

Ancient Greek Armor and Weapons

Archeologists have learned a lot about Greek armor and weapons by looking at scenes that were painted on pottery. The picture on this page is from a painting on a vase. It shows two Greek armies marching toward each other. The boy in the middle is playing a kind of flute. Soldiers marched in time to the music. Notice the helmets the soldiers are wearing. They have crests of horsehair on top. Greek soldiers put colorful crests on top of their helmets to make themselves look more frightening and fierce when they went to war.

A scene painted on an ancient Greek vase

Most of the armor and many of the weapons in ancient Greece were made from a gold-colored metal called bronze. The Greeks used bronze to cover things they made with wood, like shields and spears. The bronze made these things stronger. The Greeks also strapped pieces of bronze armor to their bodies to protect themselves when they were fighting.

To protect his upper body, a hoplite wore a breastplate. A breastplate was made up of two bronze plates, one in front and one in back. The plates were joined together at the sides by leather

This actor is dressed as a Spartan soldier wearing a bronze helmet.

straps. A hoplite also wore bronze leg guards, called greaves, to protect his legs below the knee. Even with this armor, many parts of a soldier's body were not protected.

Hoplites had two kinds of weapons. Their most important weapon was an iron-tipped spear. A hoplite would thrust his spear into the body of an enemy soldier. Hoplites also had iron swords for hand-to-hand fighting up close.

31

War with Persia

As you have learned, the Greek city-states often fought against each other. But soon after 500 B.C., they banded together to fight an enemy from outside Greece. That enemy was Persia.

The Persians had built a powerful empire in Asia. Now they came sweeping across Asia Minor toward Greece. (Asia Minor is across the Aegean Sea from Greece. It is where Troy was located.)

The Persians swept across Asia Minor toward Greece.

Persia was very large and powerful. The Greek city-states were much smaller, and they didn't have nearly as many people.

No city-state could stand up to Persia alone. The Greek city-states would have to band together to defeat the Persians. They would also have to find ways to outsmart the enemy.

In 490 B.C., the Persians and the Greeks fought an important battle at a place called Marathon. Marathon was a narrow valley near Athens. When the two armies met to fight, it was clear that the Persian army was much bigger than the Greek army.

The Greek commander thought of a clever plan. He stretched his small army out in a thin line. Then he ordered the middle part of his army to attack. The Persians thought the Greeks were crazy to send such a small number of men to fight. But as the Persians came forward to meet the Greeks, the Greek commander told the soldiers on the far left and on the far right to attack. Soon the Persians were surrounded as the Greeks moved in on them.

This was a smart thing to do, because the Persians' favorite weapon was the bow and arrow, and bows and arrows weren't very useful when the enemy was close. These weapons were no match for the strong spears of the Greeks, who were used to fighting up close, so the Persians turned their backs and fled.

Persian soldiers with bows and arrows

This early victory did not end the fight with Persia. The Greeks were at war with Persia for another 11 years, until 479 B.C. In the end, though, the Greeks were able to beat the Persians.

The Persian Wars happened a long time ago. But the Greek victory was very important because it meant that the Greek city-states, and Greek ideas such as democracy, were able to live on.

Chapter Summary

In this chapter, you learned about war in ancient Greece. Artifacts such as armor and painted pottery have taught us a lot about how wars were fought. Greek foot soldiers wore armor made of bronze and fought with spears and swords. Soon after 500 B.C., the Greeks came together to defend themselves against powerful Persia. The Greek victory in the Persian Wars allowed the city-states, and Greek ideas, to live on. In the next chapter, you will learn about some of the thinkers of ancient Greece and how their ideas changed the world.

Chapter Four

Great Thinkers of Ancient Greece

Questions this chapter will answer:

- **Who was Socrates?**

- **What new way of thinking did the Greeks invent?**

Most ancient Greek cities had a public meeting place in the center of the city. It was called the agora, which means "gathering place." In Athens, the agora was a grand square. In the middle of the square was a market where people could buy food, wine, and goods like pottery.

There were large, splendid public buildings on two sides of the square. The other two sides had covered walkways where the people of Athens could meet and talk.

This temple was one of the public buildings that stood alongside the agora in ancient Athens.

The ancient Greeks liked to talk about many things when they gathered in the agora. They especially liked to talk about ideas. They were very curious about nature and about people. How did the world begin? Why do people act the way that they do? How should people live if they want to be happy? Thinking and talking about questions like these is called **philosophy**.

The thinkers who tried to answer these questions were called **philosophers**. This is a Greek word that means "lover of wisdom."

37

Many Greek philosophers were also early scientists. Let's meet some of these thinkers and find out about their ideas.

A Thinker Named Socrates

One of the wisest thinkers in all of history was an Athenian named Socrates. Socrates did not look very impressive. He wore plain clothes and went barefoot, even in winter. He was not interested in money, fame, or power. But he was very interested in asking hard questions like "What is truth?" and "What is the right thing to do?"

This ancient Greek sculpture shows what Socrates might have looked like.

Socrates knew that these were hard questions. When people tried to answer his questions, he would often ask more questions. He asked questions to help people think carefully. He wanted them to try to discover answers for themselves. Socrates soon had a group of students who listened to him and learned from him.

Even in Athens, a city of new ideas, asking too many questions could get a person in trouble. Many people didn't like the way Socrates questioned everything.

When important men heard their ideas being questioned or challenged, they became angry.

When Socrates was an old man, some important men had him arrested, and he was put on trial. Socrates was accused of not honoring the gods and of being a bad influence on the city's youth. He was found guilty and was sentenced to death.

Socrates could have escaped the death penalty by agreeing to leave Athens forever, but he chose not to go. He stayed in Athens to stand up for his ideas, and he accepted the city-state's right to put him to death. The prison guards gave him a cup of poison from a plant called hemlock. Socrates calmly drank the poison and died.

This painting shows Socrates as he is about to drink the hemlock.

A New Way of Thinking

Greek philosophers like Socrates believed that people could discover answers to big questions through the power of their own minds. This was a new way of thinking. Before the Greek philosophers, people looked to the gods and myths to help them understand the world. Greek philosophers tried to understand the world by thinking logically about it. This is called **reasoning**. Today, scientists use reasoning to help them make new discoveries.

This painting shows Aristotle walking with his teacher, Plato.

Some philosophers, like Socrates, were mostly interested in problems of human life. Others were curious about nature. They looked closely at the earth and sky, and at plants and animals, trying to understand how nature worked.

Some Greek thinkers tried to understand the world through math. A thinker named Pythagoras discovered many of the rules of geometry, which is the study of shapes such as squares and triangles. Historians think he was the first person to suggest that the world was round.

Other Greek thinkers looked up at the sky and asked questions about the stars and the planets. A scientist called Hipparchus made maps of the sky. He named more than 800 stars.

One of the greatest Greek thinkers was Aristotle. Like Socrates, Aristotle thought a great deal about the best way for people to live. But he wrote about many other things in the world. He was especially interested in plants and animals. Aristotle wanted to organize what he learned. He created names for groups of animals, such as "animals that breathe air" and "animals that live in the water."

These Greek thinkers laid strong foundations for modern scientists. They showed the importance of numbers. They mapped the stars and planets. They created names for groups of plants and animals that scientists still use today. Most of all, they set an example of asking questions and answering them through observation and careful reasoning.

Chapter Summary

In this chapter, you met some of the great thinkers of ancient Greece. Socrates encouraged people to ask questions and to think for themselves. He stayed true to his beliefs even though his beliefs cost him his life. Aristotle and other Greek philosophers also tried to understand the world by asking questions and thinking carefully to discover the answers. This new way of thinking led to many discoveries, and it influenced the way scientists look at the world today.

You have seen that the ancient Greeks were famous for new ideas. In the next chapter, you will learn about Alexander the Great, who took these ideas and helped to spread them far beyond Greece.

Chapter Five

Alexander the Great and the Spread of Greek Ideas

Questions this chapter will answer:

- **Who was Alexander the Great?**

- **How did Alexander win an important battle in India?**

- **How did Alexander spread Greek ideas?**

Look at this picture of an ancient Greek coin. The coin shows a Greek man on a horse attacking an elephant. How could that be? There were no elephants in Greece!

An ancient Greek coin

But there *were* elephants in far-off India. Did a Greek army go all the way to India? Yes, it did. The army was led by a young man named Alexander the Great. In 334 B.C., Alexander set out to conquer the world. In this chapter you'll find out more about this amazing leader and how he spread Greek ideas far and wide.

Alexander the Great

Alexander was born in Macedonia, which was north of Greece. His father, Philip, was the king of Macedonia. Alexander and his father loved everything about Greece, especially Greek art and ideas. In fact, Alexander's teacher when he was a boy was the famous Greek thinker, Aristotle.

Alexander the Great

When Alexander was 18, his father brought the Greek city-states into his kingdom. This is how it happened.

Remember how the Greeks worked together to defeat Persia? This friendly spirit didn't last. About 50 years after the end of the Persian Wars, Athens and Sparta began a long war with each other. Other city-states joined on either side. While the Greeks were weak from fighting each other, King Philip entered Greece, defeated the city-states, and brought them under his control.

Philip died soon after he brought the Greeks together, and his son Alexander became king. Alexander was only 20 when he came to power. He moved as fast as lightning. He quickly ended trouble in one of the Greek city-states. Then he turned his attention to the rest of the world.

This picture shows Alexander riding on his horse as he takes control of Egypt.

Alexander led the Greeks across Asia for 11 years. He defeated Persia, and parts of Egypt and India, too. Soon he had built an **empire** (a huge area controlled by one ruler). You can see how big his empire was on the map on the next page.

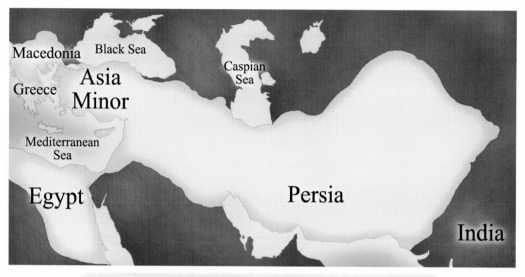

Alexander's empire is shown in yellow on this map.

Fighting an Army of Men on Elephants

Alexander fought one of his most difficult fights in India. The leader of the Indian army was called King Porus. His army was much larger than Alexander's army, and it included elephants. Alexander's men rode horses. Neither the men nor the horses had ever seen elephants before and were afraid of them. This made it hard for Alexander's army to attack.

Alexander had a clever idea. He brought some elephants to the camp so that his men would get used to them. Then, when the battle started, Alexander sent a small group of men running toward the other army's elephants. The men waved their arms and made loud noises as they ran.

The noise and movement startled the elephants, and they began to run, stepping on everyone who got in their way. This created great confusion. The Indians lost control of the elephants and the fight. And Alexander's army won.

Alexander's soldiers ran right at the enemy's elephants in India.

Alexander died four years later, in 323 B.C. He was only 33 years old, but he had created the biggest empire the world had seen.

Spreading Greek Ideas

As he created his huge empire, Alexander spread Greek ideas wherever he went. Because of this, Greek ideas lived on, even after Alexander's death. One way that Alexander spread Greek ideas was by building Greek-style cities all over his empire. Alexander's cities had temples and markets like those in Athens. Many Greeks came to live in these cities, and they brought Greek ideas, art, and the Greek language with them.

The most famous city that Alexander built was named Alexandria. Alexandria was in Egypt, close to the Mediterranean Sea. It became an important center of trade because it was near the sea. For hundreds of years it was also a center of learning. Its huge library held more than half a million books. It was the largest library in the ancient world.

After Alexander's death, his empire was broken up into three pieces. Greece and Macedonia became one kingdom. Part of Asia became a second kingdom. And Egypt became a third kingdom.

Eventually, all three kingdoms were defeated by the Roman Empire. But Greek ideas did not die out. The Romans admired Greek myths, art, and philosophy, just as Alexander had, so they adopted these Greek ideas as their own.

Chapter Summary

In this chapter, you learned about Alexander the Great. Ancient coins and other artifacts show how far Alexander traveled as he built his huge empire. In India, he won a battle against an army that included elephants. Alexander helped spread Greek ideas, which were later adopted by the Romans. In the next chapter, you will learn more about how Greek ideas continue to influence us today.

Chapter Six

Ancient Greece Today

Questions this chapter will answer:

- Do you speak Greek without knowing it?

- How are the plays that we watch today like the plays of ancient Greece?

- How are our ideas about government inspired by the ancient Greeks?

Where do you think this building is located?

Look at the building in the picture. Can you guess where this building is located?

You won't find this building in Greece. You will find it in Washington, D.C. It is the building where the Supreme Court meets. The Supreme Court is the highest court of law in the United States.

The people who designed this building loved ancient Greek temples and copied many things about them. Look at the columns at the front of the building. Notice the sculptures just underneath the roof. They may remind you of the Parthenon, the temple we explored at the beginning of this book.

You can find Greek-style buildings all over America. Look especially at banks, libraries, museums, and schools. These buildings are just one example of how the ancient Greeks have influenced us. Let's look at some other kinds of examples.

Speaking Greek

Did you know that many of the words we speak are from Greek? Some examples are "air," "hero," and "poet." A long journey is an "odyssey," which comes from one of Homer's poems. A "marathon" is a long race. That word comes from a Greek story about a messenger who ran a long way to bring news of the victory at the battle of Marathon.

These runners are finishing a marathon. Our name for this kind of race comes from Greek.

Many words that have to do with learning come from Greek, including "biology," "mathematics," and "school." Even the word "alphabet" is Greek. It comes from the first two letters of the Greek alphabet, "alpha" and "beta."

In addition to Greek words, Greek poems and stories live on today. Many students read Homer's poems, the *Iliad* and the *Odyssey*, in high school and college. Younger students often read Aesop's Fables, which also come from the Greeks.

α β

Alpha and beta, the first two letters in the Greek alphabet

Greek myths and stories have inspired many writers. In fact, you could say that an ancient Greek named Herodotus inspired this book because he was the first person to write about history.

On with the Show

Did you know that the kinds of plays we watch today come from ancient Greek plays? The Greeks invented drama. They created the two basic kinds of plays we still enjoy — comedies (funny plays with happy endings) and tragedies (serious plays with sad endings). Greek plays were often stories about the gods and goddesses. They were also about ordinary people. Actors played people who had adventures. A chorus, or group of men, spoke to the audience about what was happening to the actors.

Many ancient Greek plays have survived to this day. We can still go see them in modern theaters.

These actors are performing an ancient Greek play.

The ancient Greeks invented theaters too. The Greeks built their theaters into the sides of hills. The theaters were shaped like bowls, with seats going up the sides of the hills. This made it possible for people far off in the back to see and hear the play. Scenery was painted on large sheets of canvas that were hung behind the actors.

This ancient Greek theater was built into the side of a hill.

Rule by the People

Our form of government started in ancient Greece. As you have learned, democracy began in Athens. The example of Athens inspired the people who started modern democracies in England and the United States.

Democracy today is not exactly the same as it was in Athens. In Athens, citizens got together to vote directly on laws and important decisions, like whether to go to war. We vote for **representatives**, like the men and women of the U.S. Congress or the British Parliament, to make most of those decisions *for* us. Also, today, women are citizens and have the right to vote. But the basic idea of democracy — rule by the people — is the same now as it was in ancient Greece.

Today Congress makes laws for the people of the United States.

Chapter Summary

In this chapter you learned about some of the ways that the Greeks still influence us today. We still build Greek-style buildings. We use Greek words and watch Greek-style plays. Our form of government started in ancient Greece.

When we look at artifacts like an ancient coin or the ruins of a temple, the world of the Greeks may seem far away. But in this book you have learned how those artifacts are connected to our lives today. In many ways, ancient Greece is still all around us.

Glossary

Word	Definition	Page
agora	a gathering place in an ancient Greek city	36
archeologist	a scientist who studies things that were left behind by people who lived a long time ago	7
armor	pieces of metal that are worn by soldiers to protect themselves in battles	14
artifact	an object that was left behind by people who lived a long time ago	9
chariot	In ancient times, a chariot was a cart that was pulled by horses.	14
chorus	a group of men in an ancient Greek play who spoke to the audience about what the actors were doing	53
citizen	a person who lives in a place and has rights there To be a citizen in ancient Athens, you had to be a free man who was born in the city.	24
city-state	A city-state in ancient Greece was like a very small country that had its own government, its own army, and its own way of life.	19

Word	Definition	Page
comedy	a funny play with a happy ending	53
democracy	a kind of government where the people vote on how the country should be run	24
empire	a huge area that is controlled by one ruler	45
immortal	able to live forever	12
myths	Greek myths are the stories that the ancient Greeks told about their gods.	12
Olympic Games	the largest sporting event in ancient Greece, where the best Greek athletes competed in sports like boxing, wrestling, and races	15
phalanx	In a phalanx, a group of soldiers line up next to each other in rows with their shields overlapping to give them extra protection.	28
philosopher	a person who studies **philosophy**	37
philosophy	thinking and talking about important questions like "How did the world begin?" and "Why do people act the way they do?"	37
reasoning	trying to understand something by thinking logically about it	40

Word	Definition	Page
representatives	people who are elected to make important decisions for their city, state, or country	55
ruins	buildings that have been partly destroyed	10
sacrifice	The ancient Greeks killed animals and gave them to the gods. This was called sacrificing the animals.	15
tragedy	a serious play with a sad ending	53

About the Author

Wendy Frey grew up in New York City, and graduated from Grinnell College in Iowa. Wendy began her career by working as an editor on shows for National Public Radio. Then, she decided she wanted to write books. She studied creative writing at Goddard College, where she received a Master of Fine Arts. Since then, she has written history books for children and young adults. She has published poetry, and is writing a novel.

Wendy's interests include painting, photography, sculpture, and travel. She has visited Asia, Europe, Africa, and Central America. She lives in San Francisco, California, with her partner, John, and her cat, Kismet.

About the Narrator

Nick Sandys has performed on stage in theaters in Chicago, New York, Dallas, London, England, and Edinburgh, Scotland. You may also have heard Nick's voice in a television or radio commercial.

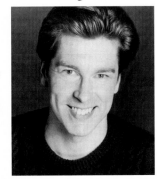

Nick is a member of Actors' Equity Association, the Screen Actors Guild, and AFTRA and is a certified fight director with the Society of American Fight Directors. Nick has an MA in English Literature and is working on a PhD. He grew up in the ancient city of York, in the north of England.

A Note to the Teacher

Start-to-Finish Core Content books are designed to help students achieve success in reading to learn. From the provocative cover question to the carefully structured and considerate text, these books promote inquiry, active engagement, and understanding. Not only do students learn curriculum-relevant content, but they learn how to read with understanding. Here are some of the features that make these books such powerful aids in teaching and learning.

Structure That Supports Inquiry and Understanding

Core Content books are carefully structured to encourage students to ask questions, identify main ideas, and understand how ideas relate to one another. The structural features of the Gold Core Content books include the following:

- **"Getting Started"**: A concise introduction engages students in the book's topic and explicitly states what they will learn.
- **Clearly focused articles:** Each of the following articles focuses on a single topic at a length that makes for a comfortable session of reading.
- **"Questions This Article Will Answer"**: Provocative questions following the article title reflect the article's main ideas. Each question corresponds to a heading within the article.
- **Article introduction:** An engaging opening leads to a clear statement of the article topic.
- **Carefully worded headings:** The headings within each article are carefully worded to signal the main idea of the section and reflect the opening questions.
- **Clear topic statements:** Within each article section, the main idea is explicitly stated so that students can distinguish it from supporting details.
- **"Summary"**: A brief Summary in each article recaptures the main ideas signaled by the opening questions, text headings, and topic statements.

Text That Is Written for Success™

Every page of a Core Content book is the product of a skilled team of educators, writers, and editors who understand your students' needs. The text features of these books include the following:

- **Mature treatment of grade level curriculum:** Core Content is age and grade-appropriate for the older student who is actively acquiring reading skills. The books also contain information that may be new to any student in the class, empowering Core Content readers to contribute interesting information to class discussions.
- **Idioms and vocabulary:** The text limits the density of new vocabulary and carefully introduces new words, new meanings of familiar words, and idioms. New subject-specific terms are bold-faced and included in the Glossary.
- **Background knowledge:** The text assumes little prior knowledge and anchors the reader using familiar examples and analogies.
- **Sentence structure:** The text uses simple sentence structures whenever possible, but where complex sentences are needed to clarify links between ideas, the structures used are those which research has shown to enhance comprehension.

For More Information

To find out more about Start-to-Finish Core Content, visit www.donjohnston.com for full product information, standards and research base.